Psycho

Inside the Mind of a Psychopath

Paul Sorensen

Paul Sorensen

Psychopath

☺ 2014 Copyright.
Text copyright reserved. Hill Tech Ventures Inc.

The contents of this book may not be reproduced, duplicated, or transmitted without direct written permission from the author.

Paul Sorensen

Disclaimer: All attempts have been made by the author to provide factual and accurate content. No responsibility will be taken by the author or publisher for any damages caused by misuse of the content described in this book. The content of this book has been derived from various sources. Please consult an expert before attempting anything described in this book.

Paul Sorensen

TABLE OF CONTENTS

INTRODUCTION	9
CHAPTER 1	12
What is a Psychopath?	
CHAPTER 2	20
The Root of the Problem	
CHAPTER 3	31
A Day in the Life of a Psychopath	
CHAPTER 4	37
Relationships with Psychopaths	
CHAPTER 5	46
Turning to Crime	
CHAPTER 6	54
Can Psychopaths be Cured?	
CHAPTER 7	65
The Psychopath Test	
CHAPTER 8	74
The World's Worst	
CONCLUSION	94

Paul Sorensen

INTRODUCTION

When you first think of the term psychopath, the first thing that comes to mind for most people is the insane, insatiable serial killer. We expect the appearance of such a depraved individual to reflect the madness without. This couldn't be more wrong.

The truth is, that charming person who holds the door open for you at work all the time, the charismatic ex you have that everyone loves, but had a bit of a mean streak behind closed doors, the guy from college who loved extreme sports, or even your surgeon – they are all quite possibly psychopaths. And, unless you know them intimately, and know what you're looking for, it's unlikely you'll ever spot it.

So, what is psychopath – really? How can you recognize it? Are they dangerous? Or do we as society actually really need them? How do we know if they're just a bad kid or could develop into something worse? This book will walk you through the history being psychopathy, how to recognize the signs, and what to do if you ever find yourself in a relationship with one. It also looks at new scientific developments and research into the condition, and profiles some of the ones that were truly evil – the world's worst. Let's hope your charming ex isn't one of those.

Thanks, I hope you enjoy it!

Psychopath

CHAPTER 1

What is a Psychopath?

What is a psychopath? You've probably heard the term before, perhaps even used it yourself. But like many people you may not know what it really means, who it's really describing.

When you first hear the word psychopath, it brings to mind violent men or sadistic serial killers, but you would be amazed at just how many psychopaths live in regular society.

Many people describe feeling something is a little 'off' with the other person, but can't put their finger on it. It's only when you delve deeper into the mind of a psychopath that you realize just how different they are.

You've probably met a psychopath in the course of your life, likely more than one. You may have even been in a close relationship with a psychopath.

Psychopathy is a personality disorder that is diagnosed by the presence of a number of different features, including manipulation of others, a lack of remorse, and no empathy for others.

Psychopaths have no moral code. They think only of themselves and care little or not at all for anyone else. It's not that they don't know what is considered right and wrong, they just don't care. They are masters at blending in, hiding their true nature. They are willing to disregard society's moral code and rules if it suits them. But, they are not psychotic. They understand the real world. It is rare for a psychopath to become psychotic, unless there is a secondary condition present.

It's a common misconception that psychopaths are mostly violent criminals. Many psychopaths do very well for themselves in society, often working in high risk or stimulating roles and jobs, such as stock brokering, extreme sports, or even lawyers. Drawn to power and admiration from others, you'll find them as CEO's, spies, test pilots, politicians, and more. They are risk takers by their very nature, and relentless in the pursuit of their goals, pushing aside anyone who gets in their way.

Psychopaths are hard wired for stimulation and sensation, and will usually have no fear or inhibitions to go along with that – a potentially lethal combination.

On top of this constant desire for stimulation, psychopaths have no moral code. They know what they are doing to other people is seen as wrong, but they simply don't care, they don't feel those pangs of guilt like the rest of us do, or feel bad for hurting the other person. They often think every day people are beneath them, and not worthy of their time or compassion. They experience no remorse, and love to control and manipulate any situation.

Because of this mindset, no psychopath is safe, even if they have never been convicted of a criminal offense.

The term psychopath was first used in the early 1800's, when doctors working in metal hospitals took note of some patients who went beyond the everyday maladies they dealt with. These patients seemed to have no morals, no sense of right and wrong. The term psychopath was formally coined in the early 1900's. Then, it was used to describe someone who had an additional mental illness or disorder, alongside the lack of a conscious.

Psychopath

In the book, The Mask of Sanity (published in 1941) psychiatrist Hervey Cleckley created the first and arguably the most influential description of psychopathy used in modern times. Further research by Robert D. Hare, a Canadian psychologist, developed a checklist for diagnosing psychopathy; a revised version of which is still used today.

Put simply, psychopathy is defined as a personality disorder, including ongoing antisocial behavior, diminished or no empathy, understanding or remorse, often coupled with bold or uninhibited behaviors and actions. Other terms you may have heard of are anti social personality disorder, or sociopathy. Historically these terms have been used along with or instead of psychopathy, and are now sometimes used to describe degrees or causes instead.

Interestingly, for many years no psychiatric or psychological organization or body has had an official diagnosis for psychopathy, and yet the term continues to be used widely in both criminal and social settings. It is also extremely popular in the press, and fictional characters. The latest edition of the DSM (Diagnostic and Statistical Manual of Mental Disorders), released in 2013, includes a definition for those who have a conduct disorder, and also have a 'callous, unemotional interpersonal style' across multiple areas of their life. This recognizes that people with psychopathy can have a more severe form of a personality disorder that also requires different responses and treatments.

Researchers in the field have noted that there is currently at least two main definitions of psychopathy, one which focuses on how you relate to others, such as lack of empathy or manipulation. The other talks more of a more persistent and serious aggressiveness and criminal behavior. Due to the implications of being labeled a psychopath, some have tried to reconcile the two.

One of the main issues with diagnosing psychopathy is that there is an ongoing disagreement as to whether it is a standalone condition itself, or instead a combination of multiple conditions, combined in different ways in different individuals.

The Hare Psychopathy Checklist is the assessment tool that most mental health professionals use to rate or evaluate psychopathy. It consists of twenty personality traits and example behaviors, and is intended to be completed via an interview and a review of records or other information available.

The checklist was developed by Robert D. Hare, a Canadian psychologist, originally for use in experiments based on his work with inmates in Vancouver. It was partially created using the clinical profile created by Hervey Cleckley. The most recent version was updated in 2003. The test gives a result of between 0 and 40, and those who score 30 or above are deemed to be a clinically diagnosed psychopaths.

Each of the items on the test are scored up to three points, from 0 to 2. As well as criminal behaviors and lifestyle, the test looks at:

- Glib and superficial charm
- Grandiosity
- The need for stimulation
- Pathological lying
- Cunning and Manipulating
- Lack of any remorse
- Callousness
- Poor behavior control
- Impulsiveness
- Irresponsibility
- Denial
- Parasitic Lifestyle
- Sexual promiscuity
- Early behavior problems
- Lack of realistic long term goals

- Failure to accept responsibility for actions
- Many short term relationships
- Juvenile delinquency
- Revocation of conditional release
- Criminal versatility

As recognized by the scoring system of the Psychopathy Checklist, whether you are a psychopath or not is dependent on several factors and is not black and white. Anyone who scores up to 30 on the test is deemed psychopathic, even though the highest possible score is 40. What we take from this is that everyone has psychopathic traits to some degree. An average person will score around 5 on the checklist, where in prison populations the average score is somewhere around 20.

The test's creators are careful to point out that it is a clinical test, and should not be used by a layperson to try to assess someone they know. Because a psychopath can be extremely manipulative and seemingly change personality as the situation requires it, an untrained person will have difficulty finding the real truth behind the layers. 'White collar' psychopaths, the ones you may suspect, will likely score lower on the test than full blown criminal personalities.

Psychopath

CHAPTER 2

The Root of the Problem

It's thought that up to 80% of psychopaths are male, and nearly all of them are heterosexual. Note that this will not stop them becoming involved in a homosexual relationship if it is beneficial to their goal.

Estimations say that up to 5% of the entire population are fully fledged psychopaths. That means there are up to 15 million in the United States alone. This isn't even counting those who exhibit only a few traits – these individuals are still able to steal, lie, cheat and even kill with no remorse.

Many people think that they'll be able to spot a psychopath, should they ever come across one. In fact, the opposite is usually true. You have likely already met at least one, and have no idea. Rather than the twisted, insane monster that we see inside our heads, psychopaths are generally intelligent and charming, often only revealing their true nature only when forced, or when they have grown bored of the relationship or situation. It's therefore lucky that they're not all serial killers, or society would have a massive problem.

Along with many conditions or behaviors that we cannot understand, many have wondered if psychopaths are born or made. Can they be helped or changed, or are they doomed from birth? From genetic and environmental causes, right through to brain disorders and simply the way you're raises, there are many different theories as to the causes of psychopathy.

Whether you are born with psychopathy and that's it, or it's something that can be controlled or even avoided is still in under intense debate today, and will likely be for a long time to come. While many exhibit disturbing behavior in childhood, not all do. Conversely, not everyone who demonstrates antisocial behavior as a child will go on to become a psychopath.

So, what do we know? We've all heard the stories about children who torture small animals, or hurt younger siblings, but there's more to it than that.

A study of eight one boys from a residential program, found that aggressive behavior, lying and stealing may all predict the development of psychopathy. Common traits in psychopathic children include:

- a mother who was also abused or neglected
- an absent father
- little or no emotional connection with the mother
- a low birth weight or complications at birth
- unusual reactions to insults or pain
- lack of any attachment to adults
- failure to make eye contact when touched
- low frustration tolerance
- sense of self impotence
- transient relationships
- cruelty towards others
- abuse of animals
- lack of remorse for hurting someone
- lack of empathy in friendships

Professor Paul Frick, from the University of New Orleans, specializes in childhood psychopathology. He has created a list of ten warning signs for children who you suspect may have psychopathic tendencies.

- Persistently hurt, bully or fight others. May also steal or vandalize other's property.
- Breaking major rules, such as staying out past curfew

Psychopath

- Show no guilt when they are in trouble for doing wrong
- Have a persistent disregard for other's feelings (not just siblings)
- Persistently do not care how they perform in school, even when expectations are made clear
- Come across as cold and unfeeling, and only use emotion to manipulate
- Do not accept responsibility for mistakes, and instead blame others
- No sense of fear, and participate in dangerous activities
- Are not bothered by threats of punishment
- Highly motivated by what they'll receive, even if the action will hurt others (eg: stealing something)

However, there is a flip side. In fact, a study by Dr. David Lykken, concluded that traits that may indicate psychopathy, such as aggressiveness, fearlessness and sensation-seeking, can be actively channeled towards behaviors society finds more acceptable. This may be where we find the extreme athletes and Wall Street psychopaths. Many psychologists believe that, if caught early enough, these tendencies can be limited, or even reversed, in children.

Overall, one common approach when studying personality disorders it to look to genetics. A study using the Psychopathic Personality Inventory (another test similar to the checklist mentioned in chapter two) found that both the factors fearless dominance and impulsive antisociality were similarly influenced by genetics, although unrelated to each other. It concluded that while genetic factors may influence the development of psychopathy, environmental factors also affect the expression of the predisposed trait. In simple terms, all lemons are yellow, but not everything that is yellow is a lemon. It is quite possible to have inherited the traits, but not express them in your personality.

Studies have also found a suggested link between a genetic mutation nicknamed the warrior gene, and psychopathy. In fact, this gene mutation featured in the storyline of Nate Haskall, a fictional character from CSI: Crime Scene Investigation. Nate was reveled to have the mutation, which some studies have linked to a predisposition to violence. Echoing real world research and opinions however, it was revealed that the CSI who eventually captured Haskall, Dr Raymond Langston, also carries the gene. It is estimated that 59% of African American men carry the gene mutation, 56% of Maori men and 54% of Chinese, compared to 34% of Caucasians.

The genes involved (MAO-A) control the production of enzymes that participate in the breakdown of neurotransmitters, such as dopamine and serotonin. They can therefore influence feelings, behavior and moods. The mutation means the person cannot control levels of these neurotransmitters in their body, and can result in violent behavior.

However, if anything, the current research has suggested that further research is needed to make any determinations. The mutation is very common, with 1 in 3 men carrying at least a shortened and therefore less active version of the gene. Some researchers consider it to be the cause of antisocial behavior in Caucasian men. Even the name 'warrior gene' is cause for concern to some people, who believe that naming a genetic mutation associated with increases in violent behavior by a positive masculine archetype just adds to the problem.

The second broad factor commonly looked at when examining behavior is environmental. A British study documented several factors that may influence the development of psychopathy. These included having a parent already in jail, being physically neglected, low family income, and little or no involvement between father and son. Other factors included poor supervision and harsh discipline, a large family, delinquent siblings, a younger mother, depressed mother, low social class and poor housing.

In other studies, research has also linked head injuries or defects with a predisposition to violence and psychopathy. Children with both early damage, or even born with damage, to the prefrontal cortex may never fully develop moral or social reasoning and understanding. Another cause may be damage to a part of the brain called the amygdala. This may impair the ability of the prefrontal cortex to understand feedback from the limbic system, a complex set of brain structures located under the cerebrum. The studies suggest this could result in violent and aggressive behaviors.

Along this line, studies have also indicated that there may be biochemical causes of psychopathy. It is not a surprise that the vast majority of psychopaths are male. Studies have suggested that a high level of testosterone, along with low levels of cortisol (a hormone released in response to stress) or serotonin (a mood regulator) may contribute to psychopathic behaviors. However, it is unclear whether high testosterone levels themselves are associated.

Other studies have found links between the acids HVA (related to dopamine) and 5-HIAA (related to serotonin) and psychopathy. Some of these studies found that people who meet the criteria for psychopathy show a greater chemical response in their brains to desired 'rewards', increasing the risk of impulsive behavior.

As well as the causes of the condition, new technology has also allowed examination of the new characteristics of psychopathy down to their language and the way their brain is wired. For example, speech and language analysis programs have been used in research that discovered that psychopathic individuals even have different speech patterns. As well as words actually used to describe situations (often crimes), psychopaths have difference in the stress or emphasis placed on words than a non-psychopath typical speech patterns.

They way that psychopaths construct a sentence, and which words are used in what order reveal more about the psychopathic mind. Computer programs are, ironically, far more skilled at detecting these patterns, as humans are heavily wired towards ignoring the words that do not matter (eg: I, to, from, it) in favor of the words in the sentence that carry more meaning to us.

A psychopath's language will also be less emotionally charged, and often will not contain anything from someone else's point of view. Even their use of more past tense than non-psychopathic people can indicate a disassociation or detachment from everyday life.

What about the term sociopath? You've probably heard it before, even used interchangeably with psychopath. They are both antisocial personality disorders, but there is a subtle difference.

We think that the term sociopathy was first introduced in the early 1900's by the psychiatrist Karl Birnbaum, and then again in 1930 by psychologist George E. Partridge, where it was first used as a sub category or alternative to psychopathy. Historically either term has been used to describe the same condition, but today there are differences.

Today, it's generally accepted that psychopaths will have some genetic and/or biological contribution to their condition, even if other factors are also present. You may describe a psychopath as someone who 'wasn't quite right', from a young age. Psychopathic tendencies may be exacerbated by circumstance, but it was there for the beginning.

In opposition, the term sociopath is now used more often to indicate someone whose condition has been brought on by an accident, injury or illness or where the condition developed as a response to extreme neglect or abuse.

Some reports also categorize other subtle differences. Where psychopaths are unable to understand regular emotions. sociopaths understand them, they are just unable to experience them themselves. Because of this, you may be more aware that someone could be a sociopath, as they tend to exhibit their true selves more often. Psychopaths hide their true personalities to the point that they are usually unrecognizable to the untrained eye. Some believe that sociopaths are also more subtle in their manipulations and schemes, and their crimes may go undetected for many years.

CHAPTER 3

A Day in the Life of a Psychopath

Although we all jump to thoughts of serial killers at the mention of psychopaths, when the term is used in a clinical setting, it refers to someone who has a set of personality characteristics, including ruthlessness, lack of empathy and conscious, but charismatic and charming. Not all of them are killers, or even criminals.

There are many myths surrounding psychopaths in today's society. Some of these are brought on by popular fiction portrayals, whether others are simply a continuation of mental illness myths in history.

Myth 1: All psychopaths are violent. Although psychopathy is a significant risk factor when predicting the likelihood of violence or violent acts, many psychopaths are not violent. Indeed, most violent offenders are not even psychopaths. While most serial killers could be deemed psychopaths, it does not follow that most psychopaths are therefore serial killers.

That said, over 50% of violent crimes overall are committed by psychopaths. This large involvement in violent crime by a relatively small group of the population may be partly the cause of their representation in the media.

Myth 2: Psychopaths are psychotic/crazy. In actual fact, psychopaths are rarely also psychotic, and will only be so if there is another condition (medical or psychological) at play. While they commit acts that seem incomprehensible to regular society, to the psychopath it all seems perfectly rational. Psychopaths are always in control, and know exactly what they're doing. Psychopaths do not experience hallucinations, or have any delusions about the real world.

Myth 3: Psychopaths are all in prison. Although overly represented in the criminal population, only 20% of prison populations are diagnosed psychopaths. Many psychopaths have no criminal record of any time, albeit some probably because they have never been caught.

Myth 4: All psychopaths are male. Although the vast majority of psychopaths are male, there are also female psychopaths. However, they tend to exhibit a more mellow version of the disorder, and may never manifest violent behavior.

Myth 5: I'll know one when I meet them. In opposition to the image first thought of when the word psychopath is mentioned, most psychopaths are not like Hannibal Lector. In fact, you've probably met at least one in your lifetime, and had no idea. Because they are masters at blending in, and are very good at manipulating you, you will have no idea of their true personality behind the facade.

So, are there any pros to being a psychopath? Depending on how you look at it, there may be. Psychopaths often make immediate decisions, and don't let fear control anything they do – simply because they don't feel it. They don't take things personally, and are highly unlikely to dwell on anything that doesn't go their way, because they never think they're to blame. They can remain cool under pressure, and are rarely influenced by outside forces.

Naturally, some jobs and professions will attract them more than others. In 2011, a British journalist named Amy Crawford ran a survey online, which allowed people to take the quiz to determine their level of psychopathy. The quiz also asked for their job and other socio-economic factors. As you most likely suspect, careers such as CEO's, lawyers and TV personalities featured top of the list. Surprisingly however, clergy was number eight on the most popular career choice ladder, below police and journalists.

While overall doctors were low on the scale, surgeons specifically were in the top ten. A prominent brain surgeon she interviewed listed his ability to remain cool under pressure and not worry about how risky the surgery is to his patient as a major plus to his career.

Some researchers believe that society actually needs psychopaths, someone to do the 'dirty work'. Psychopaths don't stop to question, or focus on what could go wrong. They're cool under pressure and, especially when motivated by a reward (even gratitude or adulation from the public) they will be extremely persistent towards meeting the goal, be that defusing a bomb or removing a tumor from your head. They may not be the type you'd want to have over for tea, but many argue that society as a whole needs them.

In fact, it has been argued that often what makes the difference between the stock market success story and the serial killer is simply a slight shift on some of the aspects of psychopathy. Perhaps one is a little less intelligent, or had a worse upbringing. Maybe the other has a little more control on their violent thoughts and actions. They are both psychopaths, but their experiences, both as children and as they move through life, coupled with their inherit physical and psychological expressions, can make the world of difference to how their psychopathy manifests.

So, what's so bad about being a psychopath, if you never act on the violent tendencies of the condition? While sometimes it would feel awfully temping to wish you didn't feel emotions, it's something that few stop to consider fully. While you're going through that terrible breakup, or you've just been fired from your job, I bet just about everyone has stopped and wished at some point they could just 'make it all go away'. But, it goes both ways. Stop for a moment and imagine never feeling happiness, never being excited at the prospect of a holiday, or celebrating because you've achieved a promotion or graduated from college. A psychopath has never experienced emotions at all, neither the devastating lows or the thrills of achievement and fulfillment.

Paul Sorensen

CHAPTER 4

Relationships with Psychopaths

Have you ever been in a relationship with a psychopath? It's something that you think you'd realize from the get go, but in fact the opposite is usually true. Psychopaths can be extremely inviting and charming, particularly when you first meet, and know exactly how to draw you in. In fact, the perpetuation of the attractiveness of the 'bad boy' may make psychopaths seem even more attractive.

Psychopaths are extremely good at reading people at a glance, and know how to manipulate them into attraction. The rate at which you find yourself falling for them may even feed their feelings of self importance and dominance over others.

If you think you may unwittingly be involved with a psychopath, here's what to look out for in the beginning of a relationship.

- Extreme charm and flattery. He'll tell you everything you want to hear, and more, especially in the beginning. He knows exactly what you want to hear and when to say it.

- You have so much in common. He will love everything that you love, and tell you that your similar backgrounds is why you're perfect for each other. Often, they will want to take the relationship to the next level quickly, before you're ready.

- He's had such a hard life. Make sure you pay attention to how he describes previous relationships, both romantic and platonic. More often than not, he will describe himself as someone who has been used or abandoned.

- Look for inflated self worth or perception. A psychopath often believes they are smarter, better, more powerful etc than anyone else.

- A history of spotty employment. A psychopath's sense of entitlement means they may have problems holding a job.

- Constantly needing stimulation. Quiet and downtime are not things that a psychopath enjoys. If someone you know needs constant stimulation and entertainment, look more closely.

- Amazing stories and pathological lies. Psychopathic personalities can crave attention and empathy, and make up all sorts of stories. Perhaps he claims to have beaten a terrible illness, or been cured of a usually inoperable cancer. Maybe he was in a terrible car accident that killed the rest of his family. Equally likely are stories of great achievements, without anything to back them up.

- Great sex. In opposition to what you may think, people who have been in relationships with psychopaths often report that their love life was extremely fulfilling in the beginning. It's just another way they try to please you. Watch out if your pleasure is made to feel more like his accomplishment than anything to do with you.

- Sudden out of character behavior. Psychopaths can sometimes make strange announcements in the middle of an everyday situation, such as suddenly saying they're leaving while cooking breakfast. More often than not, they will then suddenly deny it was ever said, or just claim it was a joke. They are likely to react extremely if you suggest they are wrong, about anything.

- Treating others unkindly. When he's not trying to make an impression on them, a psychopath will rarely have time for the feelings of anyone else. Watch how he treats waitresses, the homeless, or even animals.

- No interest or emotion/empathy. Psychopaths will not be interested in the pain or trauma of anyone else, and if they are not trying to manipulate the situation, could care less about other's misfortune. Try asking them to explain an emotion, for example 'What does sadness feel like for you?". A psychopath is generally unable to give anything but a superficial answer. As Dr. Robert Hare once put it, they know the notes but cannot hear the music.

For the psychopath, the sole goal of your relationship is to suck you in, a challenge for him. You think you've finally met the love of your life, but once you're sucked in, he's lost interest. You are only useful for as long as you can give him something, be that a sense of power and control, or perhaps money or property.

Once this happens, there is no incentive for them to control their true nature, and you start to see the monster behind the man. Where once you were the center of his universe, now you will be given only enough to keep you to continue to try to salvage the relationship. If you haven't already recognized the relationship for what it is, you'll quickly find yourself accepting worse and worse behavior from him.

Particularly because you have no idea what you did wrong, you will often find yourself bargaining, or accepting ridiculous stories or pleas that you would have never listened to in the beginning. Fearful of losing your perfect match, you stay, still holding onto that ideal from the beginning of the relationship. Even if you find out he's cheating on you, you may blame yourself for not being enough for him.

Finally, when you realize the entire relationship was never real from the beginning, the psychopath will quickly discard you and move on, leaving you to pick up the pieces. As well as psychological and emotional damage, they may also leave you in a financial mess or with damaged relationships with others who were close to you.

You may be devastated with how easily he has thrown your relationship aside, but you see, psychopaths value other humans as much as they would an old pair of socks, or any other object that has reached the end of its usefulness. There was never any true love or sentiment on their side, and when you are no longer useful they will move on just as quickly as they started.

But, you still need to be careful. Just because the relationship is over, it does not mean they will not continue to try to manipulate you. It's even common for a psychopath to stalk you, or try to destroy a new relationship you have with another. You are seen only as a possession or conquest to them, and not a person with feelings and rights of your own. You may receive threatening emails, or he may contact new people in your life. Remember how he talked about his exes when first dating you? You may well have now become the crazy ex who won't leave me alone to his new conquest.

Once you do escape, even though you may feel a burn for revenge, the best approach is to just move on and try to avoid or ignore contact from the psychopath wherever possible. Even if you do attempt (and even succeed) at revenge, it is unlikely to have any lasting consequent or impact on the psychopathic personality – they simply do not care about anything or anyone else enough. In fact, they may even congratulate themselves on 'breaking you'.

Any attention, even negative attention will re-engage their attentions and open yourself to more mind games. Rather than attract their attention again and invite them to finish what they started, however much it hurts at the time, simply walk away and take steps to mend your psyche and other relationships.

Many victims of psychopaths blame themselves for what occurred. You may have felt something was a bit off, but not have been able to pinpoint what was going, and now blame yourself for all that occurred. This can also happen simply because you cannot comprehend the level of ruthlessness and manipulation from a psychopath, all for what may seem a relatively minor goal from your point of view. If nothing else, remember that the encounter was planned and plotted from the beginning, and nothing you did can change that. Psychopaths are masters at drawing you in, and are masters of disguise.

Psychopath

CHAPTER 5

Turning to Crime

It's important to note that not all psychopaths are criminals. However many aspects of the condition lend themselves to criminal behavior, and when it does it's often of the worst kind. Psychopaths are deceptive, self centered and lack any empathy, are manipulative and show no remorse. The same charm and manipulation that could lead you to voting for someone when a psychopath runs for office is equally effective in convincing you to follow them home from the club, or come inside for a nightcap, when you normally wouldn't in that situation.

Although they make up only 1-5% of the population, psychopaths commit a comparatively higher level of the serious and violent crimes. It's estimated that up to 10 to 15 percent of offenders, and up to 20 percent of the general prison population are psychopaths. Often, a trained eye can even tell the difference between a crime committed by a psychopath and one by a 'normal' person, just by the crime scene.

Compared to regular offenders, psychopaths also have a much higher rate of recidivism. This means that they are far more likely to offend more than once, and continue to offend even if they were caught and were sent to prison before.

Identifying whether or not a psychopath committed the crime can be important, and it can change the whole way the case is managed and the suspect pursued. For example, most people (even those who commit terrible acts) would have a problem with harming a small child. A psychopath cannot feel any emotions linked to this act, and as such would act very differently.

Also, if a psychopath does commit murder, then it is likely the crime was well thought out and planned, and not as a result of a sudden loss of control or lashing out. This can make them all the much harder to catch.

Because of a psychopath's unique psychological makeup, a crime can play out very differently than if law enforcement officers were dealing with someone without the condition. Being aware of the likelihood of the suspect being psychopathic can also change interview techniques and investigation methods. A lack of understanding of the unique requirements of dealing with a criminal psychopath can lead to disastrous results.

From the very beginning of responding to a crime or criminal act, a psychopaths actions and thought processes need to be examined. For example, law enforcement or negotiators should not rely on a psychopathic offender to ever meet obligations or agreements made. A psychopath is unlikely to end the crime in any other way than was originally planned, if at all possible. It is highly unlikely they will have any empathy for the victims. In fact, in some cases the psychopathic offender has been known to continue to make ransom demands long after their victim was already dead.

Of course, ever the master manipulator, this continues if brought in for interviewing or captured. Just because someone claims the crime happened because they lost control and exhibits much remorse, it does not mean that they are not a psychopath. It simply means the offender knows exactly what to say to influence the discussion. Even skilled officers with years of interrogations under their belt can quickly lose control of a interview with a skilled psychopath.

Opened ended questions work well, if the investigating offer can keep their cool. Often, a psychopath will not be able to resist the opportunity to brag about their crimes, and perhaps inadvertently give law enforcement officers a small tidbit of information they can use. Suggesting that they were the hardest case that the unit has ever had to work on, or comments on the amount of media attention they are likely to receive can be praise that a psychopath can't resist commenting on.

It's also key to remember that a psychopath will lie, and lie often. They will even include inconsequential lies that impact nothing, simply because they want to. These lies can be extremely difficult to detect, as the usual signs of anxiety or stress that accompany a normal person's lies are absent.

Unlike with regular interrogations, there is no point trying to bond with a psychopathic offender, or to find something in common. A psychopath's world is strictly about them; they do not care about anyone else's feelings or interests.

Psychopathic criminals may also bring up other subjects for discussion, or indeed start talking about the interviewing officer and their colleagues instead. It's important that the interviewer keep the interview on track, while still inflating the offender's ego , perhaps by saying that they hadn't thought of that, and will discuss it later. Only by allowing a psychopath to continue talking for a long period of time do mistakes and inconsistencies slip in.

Comments or suggestions that the psychopath think of the victim's family and the impact on others will fall on deaf ears. As much as it may pain people to do so, the best results are often gained by instead complimenting the 'criminal mastermind', and entreating on them to share their success. If any consequences of their behavior must be shared, they should be kept as minimal as possible.

Finally, if they are caught and brought to justice, a psychopath's ability to manipulate the situation and quickly read others to learn how they should act, comes into play again. This can often result in a reduced sentence, or even a bond being issued instead. When convicted, research has shown that criminals identified as psychopaths are more than twice as likely to be released than those who do not exhibit the condition. This carries through to parole boards, where they are also more than twice as likely to be granted parole, even though their criminal acts are often considered worse and longer lasting than other offenders.

Just as many psychopaths are not criminals, many are not violent. Those that are however, are generally worse than any other type of offender. In addition, the chance of them offending over and over again is much higher. The criminal acts of psychopaths are generally more complex and involved, and can include a variety of acts. When psychopaths are criminals, they are overall more violent altogether than non-psychopathic offenders.

A major part of psychopathy is the desire for power, and to be in control at all times, and this features in the types of crimes psychopaths are involved in as well. Psychopaths are very heavily over represented in violent crime. The type of violence psychopaths engage in is also different than that of other criminals. It is more likely to be motivated by a specific goal or reward that the psychopath wants. For example, they view a kidnap victim as a means to an end to recoup a ransom. They commonly stalk their victims, planning the crime for weeks, or even months. Psychopaths very rarely commit crimes of passion. If they do commit violent crimes against another person, there is more likely a high degree of sadism involved. Psychopaths feel no empathy or remorse from hurting another individual, and will readily do this if they deem it necessary to achieve their goal.

For those psychopaths who are not violent, there is still a wide range of crimes to chose from. Theft and fraud are common, as are a number of 'white collar crimes'. We already know that there is likely a large number of psychopaths working in positions of power in large companies and organizations.

Just think for a moment about the skills psychopaths have that can aid their rise to power in such an organization; focus solely on achieving their goal, no matter what the cost; not caring who you step on to reach the top; the ability to charm everyone you meet; able to quickly read any situation and react appropriately; never feeling guilty or empathic towards actions that may have a negative effect on someone else. Psychopaths also never stop to worry they've done the wrong thing, they don't beat themselves up about a decision or live in the past. When you stop and think about it, the demands of many high flying jobs would benefit from these abilities.

Psychopath

CHAPTER 6

Can Psychopaths be Cured?

What rehabilitation options exist for psychopaths? Many believe that there is no hope at all, that psychopathy is completely incurable. They believe that personality disorders (psychopathy and others) are so deeply ingrained into an individual that they cannot be modified or changed, even with therapy.

In fact, many who are intimately involved with a psychopath are conditioned to believe that any problems in the relationship are their fault. The loved one will often undertake therapy, group support or counseling, to no avail. They may experience denial, and tell themselves that one day the 'real personality' from the beginning of the relationship will return. In actuality what they are seeing now is the real personality, the early days were classic psychopathic manipulation and charm.

With other personality disorders, although they are equally ingrained in the psyche, most believe there is a possibility for treatment and change, if the behavior is causing problems in the individual's life, and they can be shown how changing may help both themselves and their loved ones.

The problem with treating a psychopathic personality lies here. The lack of empathy for others and lack of remorse, coupled with thrill-seeking behavior and no fear of any consequences makes this approach impossible. They have no fear of what consequences their behavior may bring, and couldn't care less about what it's doing to you; therefore there is no motivation to induce change.

If you can find a reason that would benefit the psychopath to change, then they may have the motivation to do so, but it would still be extremely difficult.

An interesting case surrounding this issue is that of neuroscientist James Fallon. Fallon is a neurologist who was researching Alzheimer's, and used healthy family members as a control, scanning their brains also. At the same time, he was reviewing scans of psychopathic murderers for a side project he was working on. Going through the scans, something caught his eye and he was concerned that a scan from one of the killers had inadvertently been put in the wrong pile.

There were no name on the scans, just identification numbers, and so Dr Fallon asked a technician to look up who the scan belonged to and place it in the right pile. When the results come back, he is so shocked that he insists the result be checked again. However, the technician is insistent and it turns out, correct. The scan that so closely matches the brain scans of the psychopathic murderers belongs to him. It is James Fallon's scan of his own brain.

After absorbing the shock accompanying this information, Dr Fallon spoke at length with colleagues, friends and relatives, and other experts, and was amazed to find out that only a small number were surprised at the result. His parents shared stories of when he was a little strange in childhood, as he grew older he recalled that some of his friends were forbidden from spending time with him. On asking current friends and loved ones, they all concurred that there had been moments in their relationship where he had done things they considered irresponsible. But, he'd grown into a successful adult, with a professional job and no criminal record.

When he analyzed his results further, it was discovered that Dr Fallon was a carrier of the MAO deficiency, or the warrior gene. On thinking, he could identify many times in his life where he'd placed loved ones (and himself) in danger, or been a jerk, simply because it didn't occur to him to think about the consequences of his actions.

He started trying to change his actions, starting with how he treated the ones closest to him. To do that, every single time he started to react or do something, he had to stop himself and force himself to rethink how he acted. His family have responded positively, even though they tell him they know he doesn't really mean his new, kinder actions – he just knows his family like it. He was amazed that this was enough for them, that he was trying. He sees it as a challenge, an intellectual pursuit. He doesn't really believe he can make anything change.

Dr Fallon attributes his success in life to his good upbringing, and recognizes how easily things could have been so different.

So, if we therefore accept that psychopathy is at least influenced by something that we are born with, a condition that literally wires our brains differently, how then should psychopaths be treated in the legal system? How do we deal with responsibility when it could be argued they had no greater control of their inability to care about killing someone than a raft of other conditions currently legally accepted to mitigate or remove responsibility.

But, by taking that path, it could be equally argued that therefore people identified as psychopaths should be removed from society immediately. Surely, it is only a matter of time before they offend, or make someone or something simply 'disappear'. Why wait for them to actually commit the act, if they are wired to do from birth.

Many scientists now believe that psychopathy exists on a gradient or spectrum, mirroring the scoring system in Psychopathy Checklist. It seems that we simply cannot know if someone will commit a violent crime, simply because they are a psychopath.

In his book Without Conscience, Dr Robert Hare asserted that psychopaths lack the basic capacity to understand other's emotions. He reports that: "Like the color-blind person, the psychopath lacks an important element of experience—in this case, emotional experience—but may have learned the words that others use to describe or mimic experiences that he cannot really understand."

In this study, his research term used EEG readings, which record electrical activity in the brain. Both psychopathic and normal volunteers were shown a string of letters, some of which were nonsense and some were real words. The time it took their brain to look at the letters and decide whether it was a real word (at which point they pressed a button) was measured. When loaded words such as 'death' flashed on the screen, normal volunteers were quicker to identify the word than with regular words such as a 'tree'. There was no difference with the psychopaths.

To Hare, this showed that for most of the population, certain words carry with them strong emotional responses and feelings. For a psychopath, it's just another word.

Usually, if you had a problem that you felt could use some assistance, you would go to a counselor or psychologist, and eventually come out the other side better equipped to deal with the problem. This is not true for psychopaths. In fact, psychopaths that undergo therapy actually have a higher rate of reoffending criminally than those who don't! Some researchers believe that this is because during therapy, the psychopath learns how to read the psychologist and in turn can now manipulate such situations better with people in authority (such as doctors, police etc) than before.

In fact, research in 2013 points to the result that psychopaths may in fact be able to 'switch on' empathy, if they want to. Usually, the switch is set to off, but we may be able to change this. Research already shows that psychopaths can care for others in certain scenarios, such as where there is something in it for them. But, it takes a concerted daily effort.

Researchers showed psychopathic criminals and a control group a video of people hurting each other. At the same time, they scanned their brains. They then asked the psychopathic group to imagine the pain with the person being hurt. Then, and only then, did they show much activity in the part of the brain related to experiencing pain. Until they were specifically asked to think about the person in pain, they showed reduced activity in this area of their brain.

The puzzle then becomes how inducing empathy in a specific controlled situation can be used to help psychopaths do something that most of us feel automatically. Is it even possible to leave empathy 'switched on'? Critics have also labeled the result as inconclusive, and commented that a neural response does not necessarily mean that the psychopath is experiencing the genuine emotion.

However, one area that has proven to be effective is treatment of children and youths, before they hit adulthood. Many mental health professionals are also extremely wary to label a child a psychopath, because of all the baggage that comes with the term and what it would mean for a child's future development.

There is currently no test to officially diagnose psychopathy in children. However a number of mental health professionals believe that it is a distinct condition and can be recognized in very young children, even preschool aged. The lynchpin seems to be the callous-unemotional traits, which researchers believe may differentiate between childhood psychopaths and those with other disorders. Along with this trait seems to come a high level of lies and manipulation. This also distinguishes children who may become psychopathic, researchers believe. Most other children, even those with serious mental problems or disabilities for example, will still care if their parent is upset with them, even if they also have the behavioral issues that leads to this. A psychopathic child will not. They simply fail to feel the embarrassment and discomfort that goes along with a scolding.

However, linking psychopathy and childhood still remains controversial, mainly because a child's brain is still developing and changing. It's also important to remember that many children go through stages in life where an undesirable behavior can manifest, only to resolve itself as the child grows and matures.

The fear among some experts is that although labeling a child as psychopathic can be extremely damaging, ignoring it can be even worse. Research into adult psychopathy has already shown that environment plays a factor, and if children who may develop psychopathy can be identified early, there may be some hope the condition can be mitigated or avoided, with the proper treatment and behavioral training. However, a parent of a child undergoing such treatment have voiced concerns over whether their child is really getting better, or they're just learning how to behave so their psychologist thinks they are.

In the 1970's, a psychiatry researcher named Lee Robbins studied a series of children, all who had been identified with behavioral issues. These studies followed each child into adulthood. The study reveal two important facts. Firstly, it was identified that nearly every child that grew into a psychopathic adult in the study was extremely anti-social as a child. Secondly, and perhaps more importantly, nearly half of those who scored high on anti-social test as a child in the study did not develop psychopathy as an adult. In other words, you could not rely on an test in early childhood to accurately predict future psychopathy. It is results such as these that give researchers hope.

Meanwhile, while experts battle over whether a psychopath can be cured or rehabilitated, the criminal justice system is left with the more practical problem of where to house the psychopathic offender. In some states, sexually violent offenders are held in mental institutions instead of prisons. However, this too raises debate. Should dangerous criminals be held in with other mentally ill patients? Finally, it's also argued that civil commitment is unfair when faced with a lifelong, pervasive mental deficiency.

One thing is clear however, even if a cure is ever found, who will volunteer for it. In the mind of the psychopath, there is nothing about him that needs fixing. Therefore, the best way to deal with psychopaths right now is to try to identify them as early as possible, and steer clear.

CHAPTER 7

The Psychopath Test

Just for Fun: The Psychopath Test—Are you one of them?

Here are the 20 traits of psychopathy according to the Hare PCL-R criteria. Give yourself a score of 0 if the characteristic does not apply to you at all, 1 if it slightly describes you, and 2 if it describes you perfectly.

Superficial charm – Are you a smooth-talker? Do you enjoy speaking in crowds, never getting tongue-tied or self-conscious? Do you speak your mind, no matter how it may affect others?

Rating: _____

Tremendous self-worth – Do you see yourself as very important? Do you believe you are superior above all other human beings? Have any of your friends (if you have any) told you that you're a tad too opinionated and overconfident at times?

Rating: _____

Tendency towards boredom – Do you hate routine? Do you crave excitement, taking risks, and doing dangerous tasks? Do you hate tedious tasks and often abandon projects mid-way because you've lost interest in them?

Rating: _____

Pathological lying – Do you think you're clever or shrewd? Do you possess a great deal of intelligence? Have you, in any instance, used your cleverness to deceive and control other people?

Rating: _____

Conning and manipulation – Do you use your skills of manipulation in order to cheat or exploit other people for personal gain? Have you ever been involved in or considered engaging in any form of fraudulent activity?

Rating: _____

Remorselessness – Do you feel nothing about the people that you've hurt or caused to suffer because of your schemes? Do you not sympathize with other people who have had bad things happen to them? Do you think anyone who's stupid enough to become your victim only deserves what they get?

Rating: _____

Shallow emotions – Do you often wonder what the fuss is all about when it comes to love and relationships? Have you never felt in love with someone, not even a modicum of affection? Do you hide your coldness and disconnect from others by maintaining a gregarious façade?

Rating: _____

Un-empathic and callous – Do you feel nothing about other people at all? Do you regard them all as useless unless you have a need for them? Do you not mind saying hurtful words to other people? Do you not consider the feelings of other people before you say or do something?

Rating: _____

Parasitic tendency – Do you prefer to live off others' works instead of doing hard work yourself? Do you intentionally manipulate others so that you can freeload off their hard-earned financial security? Would you rather get easy money from someone else than tax yourself in your career?

Rating: _____

Short temper – Are you easily annoyed or angered by the slightest mishap? Do you tend to show your anger or impatience easily? Do you resort to threats or even verbal and physical abuse when something or someone displeases you?

Rating: _____

Promiscuity – Have you had a lot of sexual partners? Have you ever maintained multiple relationships at the same time? Do you treat your partners coldly and almost impersonally, and regard sex only as a means to boost your ego?

Rating: _____

Aimlessness – Do you find it hard to develop long-term goals for yourself? Or, do you make plans but fail to follow through on them?

Psychopath

Rating: _____

Impulsivity – Do you tend to do things depending on your moods and whims? Are you easily tempted to try something that interests you and then plunge ahead without making any plans? Are you easily frustrated when things don't go your way?

Rating: _____

Childhood misbehavior – When you were a child, did you frequently get in trouble because of different misbehavior, such as lying, thievery, bullying, or vandalism? Have you ever run away from your home and family?

Rating: _____

Juvenile delinquency – When you were a teenager, did you have a record of criminal activity (convicted or otherwise)? Did you manipulate or bully other people, or engage in more serious crimes in your youth?

Rating: _____

Irresponsibility – Do you perpetually fail to keep your word and honor your promises to other people? Do you fail to meet deadlines and adhere to schedules simply because you can't push yourself to care about them?

Rating: _____

Laying blame on others – When things go wrong, do you have the tendency to immediately point a finger at other people? Do you think that your decisions are always right? Are you always on the defensive when people point out your mistakes? When you get blamed for something, do you respond by launching an antagonistic tirade that points the blame in an entirely new direction?

Rating: _____

Multiple failed marriages – Have you been married and divorced numerous times, or do you at least have several failed long-term relationships? Have your relationships failed because you couldn't commit to your partner long enough, and you ended up getting bored halfway through the relationship?

Rating: _____

Multiple crimes – Have you been engaged in different types of crimes? Do you pride yourself on your criminal activities? Have you committed any crimes that you got away with?

Rating: _____

Revocation of parole – Have you been in and out of jail numerous times? Have you reverted to criminal behavior, which resulted in the revocation of your parole?

Rating: _____

Scoring and Diagnostics

So, are you a psychopath or not? Psychopaths usually score 30 or above in the Hare-PCL-R diagnostic test, with 40 being the "perfect" stereotypical psychopath, while a "normal" individual with no psychopathic tendencies at all will score 5 or less. Non-psychopathic individuals with criminal backgrounds will likely have scores of around 22 and above, but no more than 30.

Another diagnostic tool is Cleckley's clinical profile for psychopathy, but the Hare PCL-R is the more widely used tool today.

Psychopath

CHAPTER 8

The World's Worst

"You have to give them hope. If you bring a human being to the brink of death, then you offer a chance, no matter how small a chance, to survive, they'll grab it. And they'll thank you for it. And then, you can do whatever you want. And believe me, I did." – Nate Haskall, CSI: Crime Scene Investigation.

It has always been the psychopathic serial killer that fascinate us more than any other, whether in real life or fiction. From famous psychopathic serial killers like Charles Manson, John Wayne Gacy, and Ted Bundy, all the way through to some of the best known movie characters. Take James Bond for instance. The series is one of the most popular movie franchise, and continues to release new films well after the original creator is dead. Did you ever stop to think that although the movies regularly feature psychopathic villains, James Bond himself is also very likely a psychopath. Reckless, intelligent, charming, involved in many relationships that are over as soon as they begin, kills with abandon – need I go on?

Perhaps the most famous fictional psychopath is Norman Bates, from the aptly named Robert Bloch novel, Psycho. A film by the same name was made in the 1960's by Alfred Hitchcock. Since then, there have been remakes and sequels, and now a TV show prequel called Bates Motel in 2013. The TV show portrays how Norman's psyche unravels through his teenage years.

As we have come to expect, both the book and the film document severe emotional abuse from Norman's mother, and the death of his father while he is still a child. As a teenager, Bates murders both his mother and her lover, and gets away with it. It has been reported that Norman Bates was loosely based on Ed Gein, an American murderer, born in 1906 and died in 1984. As well as murders, Gein exhumed corpses and took the bodies home, where he then tanned them and made items from their skin and body parts.

One of the most famous psychopathic killers from the twentieth century was Charles Manson. It should be noted that as well as exhibiting all the qualities of a psychopath, it's possible that Manson also has a mental illness that affects his perception of reality.

Mason was born in 1934, to a sixteen year old mother. During his childhood, Mason was often neglected. It's rumored that he was once even sold to waitress in return for a jug of beer. However we remain unsure about many of the facts from Manson's childhood, as they come from stories that he himself told journalists.

His mother was reportedly regularly absent for weeks at a time in his first years, during which time he was looked after by his grandmother and aunt. When Mason was five, his mother was convicted for robbery and went to jail. He moved in with his aunt and uncle, only to move back in with his mother when she was released three years later.

As Mason grew up, he moved often between temporary homes, with his mother. He was caught stealing at age nine and sent to a reform school. This happened again when he was twelve years old. When he was thirteen his mother tried to put him in foster care. There was no one who could take him, and so he was instead placed in a boys home. By the next year, he had run away and tried to return home to his mother, but was rejected.

After this, he lived on his own and survived by stealing. This meant that he spent time in a number of juvenile detention centers and facilities across multiple states. During one of his last placements, he held a razor blade to the throat of another detainee and raped him. He was then placed in a correctional facility in Ohio, and it is here that he learned to read and was deemed more co-operative than any of his other placements.

When Mason was twenty, he was paroled and spent time living with various family members. He married when he was 21, and had a son. He continued his life of crime, and when his son was born, Mason was in jail for auto theft. He and his wife divorced while he was still incarcerated.

He was released in 1967, and moved into an apartment in Berkeley. He then married Mary Brunner, and they moved into together. It was here that we start to see the mass charm and manipulation side of Mason.

Soon after, there were eighteen other women also living in the apartment, and Mason started gathering followers, both male and female. He moved them all to a ranch in California, where he made several of the female group members have sex with the owner of the ranch in return for allowing them to live there. Later, they moved to another ranch in Death Valley, where he told the owner they were musicians.

Mason often preached to his group, telling them of a racial holocaust that would start with black people rebelling against white people. He named this Helter Skelter, after the Beatles song. He also interpreted other lyrics from the same album as prophecies of the event. He even compared his own life to that of the Book of Revelations, and called himself Jesus Christ.

Lead by Mason, the group began to plan to start the prophesized war by releasing an album would trigger Helter Skelter. Murders of white people by black people would start the war, and a split between racist and non-racist whites would result in their self destruction. Mason and his 'family' would simply wait out the war, and then take power themselves at the end.

The group was told that a record producer named Terry Melcher was going to visit the ranch and hear their own album, designed to trigger the predicted race wars. However he never ended up arriving, and so Mason went uninvited to Melcher's last known address. At the time, he had moved on and the director Roman Polanski lived there with actress Sharon

Tate. He was met by a photographer friend of Tate's, who asked him what he wanted. He was told by residents of the house that the man he was looking for did not live there, and Mason eventually left, only to return that evening and ask the owner of the property, Rudi Altobelli where he could find Melcher. Altobelli lied and said he did not know, and requested that Mason did not disturb his tenants, Tate and Polanski.

Terry Melcher did eventually visit the ranch and heard the group sing, but it went no further. So, by June of 1969, Mason started saying that they may have to help the blacks start the war. He told Charles Watson, a central member of the group, to organize financing for the venture. He did this, by defrauding a black drug dealer named Bernard 'Lotsapoppa' Crowe. This was met with a threat from Crowe to kill everyone at the ranch. Manson retaliated by shooting Crowe at his apartment in July, 1969. Mason believed he had killed Crowe, but in fact he survived.

Later that same month, Mason sent other family members to the house of Gary Hinman, trying to convince him to give a suspected inheritance to the group. The three members held Hinman hostage for two days. Mason made an appearance himself with a sword to slash his ear, and after this one group member stabbed Hinman to death. They set the scene to mimic a political murder, and drew a Black Panther symbol on the wall in blood.

In August, the group member who had murdered Hinman was arrested, caught driving the victim's car, and the police recovered the murder weapon from the car. Two days after the arrest, Mason told his family members that 'Now is the time for Helter Skelter." He told Charles Watson to take three female group members back to Melcher's previous residence and kill everyone there as brutally as possible. At the time, the now heavily pregnant Sharon Tate lived at the house with her former lover and friend, Jay Sebring, a friend of her husband, Wojciech Frykowski and his lover, Abigail Folger. Roman Polanski was working in London.

After midnight on the 9th of August, 1969, the group backed their car down to the bottom of the hill that lead to the residence, and then walked back up to the house. Rather than risk an alarm, they climbed over an embankment into the grounds. At the time, a car driven by an eighteen year old, Steven Parent passed by. Watson held up the car and shot Parent four times in the chest. He then ordered the other members to help him push the car further up the driveway. The group then removed a window screen and entered the residence, leaving member Linda Kasabian to keep watch.

Frykowski, who was sleeping on the couch and was woken by the group, was first to be attacked. Following this, they found the others and assembled them all in the living room and started to tie them up. When Sebring protested against the treatment of Tate as she was pregnant, he was shot, and then stabbed.

Frykowski managed to break free and struggled with a member of the group. As he was fighting his way out the door, Watson hit him with the gun multiple times, and then stabbed and shot him also.

At this time, Kasabian came back up to the house in response to the sounds, and tried to stop the others by telling them she heard someone coming, falsely.

Folger then managed to escape and fled outside, where she was caught by a group member. Watson then stabbed her 28 times. Frykowski also staggered across the lawn, where he was caught and stabbed 51 times.

Still inside the house, Sharon Tate pleaded with the group to save her baby. Her pleas fell on deaf ears and she was also stabbed to death. The group again staged the scene using Tate's blood and fled.

The next evening, the same group along with two others, left again under Manson's instructions. He was unhappy with the panic of the victims from the previous night and wanted to show the group how it was done. After some time, they arrived at the home of Leno and Rosemary LaBianca. Leno was a supermarket executive, and Rosemary a dress shop owner. The victims were again restrained and murdered by stabbing. They once again set the scene and left. Manson had hoped to kill another that night, but left his group members to commit the act alone. Here again, Kasabian deliberately knocked on the wrong door, causing the group to forget the plan and leave.

After an investigation and lengthy trial, where Kasabian was granted immunity in return for her testimony, a guilty verdict was returned on 29 March, 1971 for all defendants, with a death penalty recommendation. Manson was also found guilty of the murders of Gary Hinman and another man who worked at the California ranch in another trial, conducted after the trial of the Tate murders.

In the Tate trial, Manson originally wanted to act as his own attorney, but this permission was subsequently withdrawn due to his behavior. There was ongoing interruptions throughout the trial, and witnesses were threatened and injured in attacks. Throughout the trial, Manson's behavior became more and more bizarre, whether this was a genuine mental illness or another manipulation technique, we will never know.

On the day the verdicts were announced recommending the death penalty, another body was found. It was never proven that the group was responsible, but a member claimed responsibility. Other bodies were then found and attributed to the group in 1972. In February of that year, the death sentences of all members were automatically reduced when the death penalty was abolished in California.

Before the end of the second trial, a reporter found Manson's mother, who had remarried and was living in the Pacific Northwest. She claimed that her son had not been abused or neglected during his childhood, and was in fact doted upon. It's unlikely we will never know the full story, or the truth of Mason's upbringing and ultimate acts of violence.

In contrast to Mason's bloody rampage, the next serial killer conducted over thirty murders and assaults over four years, before eventually being captured. We will never know the true number of his victims, which could be much higher.

Theodore Robert Bundy was born on November 24, 1969. Nicknamed Ted, he used his good looks and accomplished skills of charisma to exploit the young girls he preferred. He would usually manipulate the situation by claiming an injury, or in opposition impersonate someone in authority, to gain his victim's trust. He would then assault and murder them in a more secluded location. Ted Bundy would often then revisit the scene of the crime and engage in sex acts with the corpse, until decomposition and attacks on the body by wild animals made this impossible. At least twelve of his victims were also decapitated, and he kept their heads as trophies. Several times, he simply broke into a house when the urge took him and he killed his victim in their sleep.

Ted Bundy was born to an unwed mother, and never knew the identify of his father for certain, although his birth certificate lists an Air Force veteran Lloyd Marshall as his father, later disputed as the biological father by his mother. There was some discussion that his father was actually his own grandfather, who abused his mother. This however has never been proven.

Bundy first lived with his grandparents, and was raised as their own. Family and friends, and even the young boy himself, was unaware that his maternal grandparents were not actually his mother and father. He believed his mother to be his sister. Bundy eventually became aware of the truth, but we do not know how. Bundy has told of a life-long resentment of his mother for this act.

Bundy's grandfather has been reported as a bigot and bully, who abused his wife, and also other family members and animals. Given that psychopathy has exhibited a genetic link, it is likely that Bundy inherited some part of his condition from his grandfather, whether through his mother or directly if the rumors of Bundy's parentage are true.

His grandmother suffered from depression, and underwent treatment with electroconvulsive therapy. Towards the end of her life, she feared even leaving the house.

Even from an age as early as three, there are reports from family members of the young Ted displaying disturbing behavior. His aunt reports awaking one day to find herself surrounded by knives from the kitchen and a young Ted smiling at her.

In the 1950's, Bundy's mother changed her surname and moved to live with cousins in Washington. It was here she married Johnny Culpepper Bundy, and Ted took his surname when he was adopted formally. They went on to have four children of their own. Although efforts were made to include Ted in family activities, he is reported to have remained at arm's length. Later reports has Ted criticizing his adopted father's lack of intelligence and ability to make money.

Bundy has later recounted differing stories to several biographers about his time growing up in Washington, but a central theme of violence and peeping on naked women runs through all accounts. He claimed that he could not understand relationships with others, and stayed alone in his teenage years by choice. However, his classmates at the time have reported that he was well liked, and so perhaps this is yet another example of a psychopath learning how to game the system.

After graduating from school, he began a relationship with a woman known by different pseudonyms by his biographers, usually using Stephanie Brooks. This relationship disintegrated in 1968, leaving Bundy devastated, and is seen as a turning point in his development. After this time, he was involved in several complicated relationships, ending up in dating both his old girlfriend Brooks and his current love interest at the same time. At a time, marriage was discussed and he even introduced Brooks as his fiancé. Soon after his however, Bundy cut off all contact immediately and when Brooks approached him to know why, he denied having any idea what she was talking about. He has related later that he simply wanted to prove he could have married her if he wanted. Once he had achieved this goal, he was no longer interested. At the same time, women started disappearing across the Pacific Northwest.

There is no agreement or strict timeline on when Bundy first attacked a woman, or indeed first killed someone, as he has changed his story many times. Times range from the late 1960's and early 1970's. Some believe he may have even started killing when he was still a teenager. From early 1974, shortly after Bundy broke it off with Brooks, young female college students began to disappear at the rate of approximately one a month.

A sketch of the attacker was released to the media, along with a detailed description of Bundy's car. Three acquaintances of Bundy, including Elizabeth Kloepfer (with whom he'd had a relationship), reported him, but detectives thought a clean-cut law student with no criminal record was an unlikely offender.

Bundy was arrested in August 1975, after he did not pull over during a routine traffic stop. The arresting officer, noticing that the car's front passenger seat was absent, decided to search the car. Inside, he found two masks, handcuffs, a crowbar, rope, and ice pick and other items for burglary. The detective remembered a similar suspect and car description from the previous reports. He was released from this arrest, but placed under surveillance. Detectives also interviewed Kloepfer, who had since called police a second time. She reported strange and threatening behavior from Bundy, as well as finding strange items in their home, reporting that she believed anything of value that Bundy owned was stolen.

Bundy sold his car to a teen in September of that year, and police then immediately impounded the vehicle. The FBI then fully searched it, and found forensic evidence linking Ted to some of the disappearances. In October, Bundy was put in a lineup, where he was recognized by witnesses from other disappearances. This time, he was freed on bail.

Over the coming months, detectives from multiple branches and locations would meet to discuss the case. They were convinced of Bundy's guilt, but wanted more hard evidence before taking the case to trial. Eventually, in February 1976, Ted Bundy stood trial for the kidnapping of one victim in a bench trial, forgoing his right to a jury. He was convicted and sentenced to one to fifteen years prison. At least once, he was caught attempting escape from the prison.

In 1977, he was extradited to Aspen to stand trial for the murder of Caryn Campbell. In this trial, he chose to represent himself, and was therefore excused from wearing the usual shackles and handcuffs. He then asked to visit the law library to research his case, and escaped out a second story window. After wandering for six days, he was noted as driving erratically, pulled over and arrested again.

Bundy was returned to prison, but the case against him began to fall apart. He could have been free in a year and a half, but against advice of friends chose to try to escape again. This time, after losing a significant amount of weight, he used a hacksaw to saw a hole through his cell's ceiling and escape into the crawlspace. Some weeks later, over the holiday period when the prison was quieter and less officers and prisoners were still there, Bundy stacked books in his bed to look like he was sleeping, and then climbed into the crawlspace. He broke through into an empty office, changed clothing, and walked out the front door. His escape was not discovered until the following day, and Bundy was already half way across the country.

Bundy eventually ended up in Florida, where he resumed stealing to survive after a single job application asked him for identification. About a week after arriving, he entered a sorority house and killed one women, attacking another three. He then attacked a fifth woman eight blocks away.

The next month, he started following and approaching girls as young as twelve. The first was foiled, but the second abduction was successful and Bundy killed her. The next week, Bundy was lacking funds and suspected police were closing in, and so he stole a car and fled. He was stopped at a state line and placed under arrest. When he attacked the officer and tried to run, he was shot at by police. The police then gave chase and arrested him. At the time, the arresting officers had no idea who it was that they'd apprehended.

Following charges for the sorority attacks, he again handled most of his own defense. A member of his appointed defense team is quoted as saying Bundy "sabotaged the entire defense effort out of spite, distrust and grandiose delusion ...Ted [was] facing multiple murder charges, with a possible death sentence, and all that mattered to him apparently was that he be in charge."

During the trial for this and other subsequent charges, Bundy was sentenced to death three times. In a final act of desperate manipulation, Bundy asked a co-worker testifying as a character witness to marry him during her testimony, taking advantage of a little known Florida law that a marriage declaration in front of a judge in court counted as a legal marriage.

When the third guilty verdict was announced he yelled to the court "Tell the jury they were wrong!" This was the one that eventually lead to his death sentences being carried out nine years later.

During his planning, crimes and trial, Ted Bundy was unusually organized and calculating. He used his ample charisma, as well as faking injury, to attract young girls, who he would then brutally attack, often returning to violate them again after death. He fought his sentence to the end, and also attempted escape several times more. After his convictions, he continued to command attention from the public and talked to multiple biographers, telling each different stories. It was noted by Special Agent William Hagmaier, a member of the FBI's Behavioral Analysis Unit, that he had a deep satisfaction in murder, that the victim became part of him and become sacred.

Finally, with all avenues of appeal exhausted Bundy agreed to reveal all to investigators. When it became clear to Bundy that no further stays would then be forthcoming as a result of this information, his supporters began to lobby for clemency. A new love interest of Bundy's and victim's families all asked for more time to give Bundy a chance to reveal more information, likely Bundy's plan all along. All were refused, and Ted Bundy was executed on January 24, 1989.

"I don't feel guilty for anything. I feel sorry for people who feel guilt." – Ted Bundy.

Psychopath

CONCLUSION

Thanks again for reading this book!

So, what do you think we should do about psychopath? Should the offenders be locked up for life, so they can't offend again? What about before they offend at all?

If we treat psychopathy as an illness that will eventually lead to violence, perhaps we will also lose the highly trained bomb squad members, or maybe a few Navy SEALS. How about the stockbrokers and surgeons? Where do we draw the line at prevention versus persecution?

Many psychopaths will never act violently, but does this mean they're not dangerous? There are rumors that key players in recent events such as Bernie Madoff may well be psychopathic, and there's no doubt that his actions caused a great deal of harm to many people. But then, what do we do about people who may be psychopathic through an acquired brain injury, or triggered by an abusive childhood.

Printed in Great Britain
by Amazon.co.uk, Ltd.,
Marston Gate.

Perhaps more grassroots research and early intervention actions are the true answer to protecting society from psychopaths.

Whatever we decide the answer is, it's likely that some psychopaths will slip through the net, using their innate abilities of manipulation and charm, and perhaps if we find a 'cure', if we stop double checking and second guessing, we'll never know we're staring them in the face, until it's too late.

Thank you,

Paul Sorensen

PS. If you enjoyed this book, please help me out by kindly leaving a review!